once upon a girl

```
'''
```

Katie Keridan

Dear Caroline,

Thank you so much for your unfailing enthusiasm and support of my poetry. I am so glad we connected, as your tarot readings never fail to speak to my soul. I hope you enjoy this book!

All the best, Katie

⌁

"Soul Recognition" and "My Moment" first appeared in
The Sand Canyon Review 2018
"The Truth of Always," "Interludes," and "Different
and Never Enough" first appeared in
Inquietudes Literary Journal 2018
"Hotel Room" first appeared in *Madness Muse Press* 2018
"Space Between" first appeared in *On Arrival*
(Eber & Wein Publishing, 2018)

ISBN-13: 978-1727705386

ISBN-10: 1727705386

For Cameron, for believing I was a writer

For Christine L,
for being the first person to ask me
when I was going to write a poetry book

For my Haven writing group
for pushing me until this was completed

For the Instagram writers who encouraged me
from the very beginning —
if you read this and wondered if I
was talking about you,
chances are, I was

For my family
for always supporting my writing

And most of all, for you, the reader —
may you know that you are not alone
in how you feel

Foreword

in this book
you hold pieces of my life
of my heart
experiences preserved in letters
and fashioned into words
these experiences are not always pretty
but they are real

pain frequently uses words as an escape route
(oh, how I know)
so be kind to yourself as you read
you never know what these writings
may stir up within you

the ending is happy
the beginning was horrific
so let's start there

once upon a girl...

I crumble under the weight of this pain
except...I don't
I just wish I could.

(what is the proper response for when the spouse
you were in the process of divorcing
commits suicide?)

if I'm so god-damned strong, why do I hurt so
much?

because being strong doesn't mean you don't
feel pain
it means you have the superhuman ability
to stay standing while every part of you gushes
blood
long after anyone else would have bled to death

*(why did I have to be the strong one? why am I
the survivor?)*

it's interesting that being empty has a feeling
"nothing" can fill you up
just as full as "something" can
hollowed, scooped out, empty rounded edges
thick and heavy and bursting at the seams
with nothingness

*(I'm not just alone...I'm alone with the secrets
of an abusive marriage that I worked so hard
to keep anyone from ever uncovering)*

some days I cry so I don't drown

it's you —
and then, it's not —
but it should be —
it always will be

*(why can't I stop thinking about him
after all these years? the timing is terrible.
my life just fell apart. then again, I'm free.)*

signs you might be healing:

when you wear perfume and it's not for
date night with him

when you wear the skinny jeans he didn't
approve of and actually go out in public

when you break out the stilettos you haven't
worn in five years and wear them to a "ladies
with no babies" meet-up group

when you feel good about all of the above

hearts can break from being dropped —
not all damage comes from being
ripped in half

*(carelessness. laziness. selfishness. there are so
many ways to hurt a heart...especially one that's
already fragile to begin with)*

Space Between

it's amazing how much space there can be
between
two things…between two definitions.
between what was and what's yet to come.
between what you're not looking at behind you
anymore
and what you're staring in the face but haven't
arrived at yet.
so many endless possibilities in the chasm
between more than friends but less than
something else.
so much space in that first flutter of your heart,
when you realize that
while it's still less than something,
it's now more than nothing.

(05/07/17)

how do you change?
sometimes all at once
sometimes one step at a time
sometimes one thought about one step
at a time
sometimes crying on your couch
not knowing what you're going to do next

*(sometimes it means accepting a job offer from
your former mentor that requires you to move
across the country, back to where
you left your heart...
California)*

"what you want is out there.
don't settle.
wait for it."

okay, that's great…
but what if I don't
know
what I want?

and then…everything changes.
falling in those clear, blue eyes
treading the waters of hopefulness
keeping my head above the fear
refusing to let it drown me.
I'm terrified to fall.
so we hold on together
afraid but still afloat

(when you get a second chance with someone,
10 years later)

the small curling fear, winding like a slow single tendril
up through my gut and around each rib
taking root in my heart and spreading to my soul
each little uncertainty
each little unknown
the swift inner chill of the frozen ice plant
that grows even while frozen
coldness extending
paralyzing the joy that didn't care
stifling, choking, cutting off, silencing
fear slows, then stops, then kills, then consumes
leaving a trail of blood-red ice.

(the first time you get freaked out about something in a new relationship)

sometimes simply standing there is the bravest
thing we do
we want to run, to crumble
to go hide in a corner until the darkness passes
we're driven to seek safety until the talons of
madness
no longer reach for us
when you know the demons are descending
— or worse, that they're already there,
walking toward you —
sometimes the most impressive thing you can
do is
merely to stand
to hold your shaking self in hand
and face in the daylight
what haunts you in the dark
to look your nightmare in the eye and see
yourself reflected back
they say nothing is as frightening as the
unknown
and that may be true
but I wonder if those who say that have ever
faced their basest selves
have ever stood there standing when before
they ran
even if it means standing alone…
which it inevitably did

the depths of the oceans were contained
in her eyes
they weren't for the faint of heart
those worried about drowning,
unsure of their skills on the high seas
but for those who braved the storms
who crested each wave that threatened
to overwhelm them
who were more afraid of missing something
than of drowning
those lucky few saw sights such as others
would never believe

*(I try to be worth — no, I AM worth
someone's time and effort)*

all I want to be
is someone's everything

*(not very feminist or independent of me, but
there you have it)*

Dear Diary…

I'm not used to writing about a boy in my diary. It's been years — over a decade. It feels good, silly, innocent, flirty, takes me back to being a teenager when all my hopes and dreams and problems seemed so huge and insurmountable and true love led to a break-up precipitated by me saying, "I think it might be better if we were just friends." I don't want that anymore, that softness, that letting someone down gently. I want to go full force, all in, and when I leave, to go out with the gale force wind of a hurricane. No more delicate rustling breezes for this bitch.

Hopefully no more leaving, either.

Different and Never Enough

you were the earth
and I was the rain
and even though I poured myself into you
it was never enough
you took and took
and I gave and gave
and I wish you would have stayed full
or that I had eventually remained empty.
but we didn't
because that wasn't the natural state for either
of us
you always wanted more
and I somehow managed to produce it.
if only we had been different
if only we'd been enough.

*(you couldn't have convinced me otherwise, I'm
sure, but I wish someone would have tried)*

I die a little
taking pieces of me to feed the fire
that keeps him warm
you don't notice that it's a slow death
when you're disappearing little by little
it's not until you reach for another piece
and realize there's nothing left
that you even notice what you've become
what you've done to yourself in the name
of love

sometimes you don't know
how alone you are
until you're surrounded
by a group of people
who've been kind enough
to take you in

(when you meet his family)

you saw me
and in your gaze
I became something
real
but when you looked away
I started to fade
— solidity slipping
jeweled colors dulling —
so I held my own gaze
and saw myself
my eyes held up my soul
and I became a new kind of real
— independent.

(the pitfalls of letting someone else define you)

silently
the shadow
slinks along behind me
slipping between the trees
black
but not quite blending
into the early morning darkness
I can sense it watching me,
wondering,
trying on what it might feel like
to be solid
to have edges that protrude
asserting, expanding
taking up space in the world
what would that be like?
I often wonder myself

*(it's so hard for me to assert myself. I don't want
to upset anyone, because people get upset
with me, and then they leave)*

and then
it happens
what you hoped for
what you dreaded
what you gave
any thought to
then tried to push
from your mind
scared to
offer encouragement
afraid to chase it away
terrified that your mind
is slowly
shaping your world

*(my mind is a beautiful, dangerous place I
respect and someday hope to understand)*

there was fire in her eyes
and ice in her soul

*(an effective combination not necessarily
associated with happiness)*

given the opportunity

the words in my blood
pour from my fingers

spilling my soul
alive on the page

and when she smiled
when she really smiled
the stars gasped and the moon blinked
and the entire cosmos shivered in anticipation
hers wasn't the smile that launched ships —
it was the kind that created galaxies

(I unexpectedly saw my smile in the mirror one day after a very long absence. I'd forgotten what it looked like, and its arrival truly stunned me)

The Truth of Always

"you," she said, her eyes glowing like two
burning meteors.
"it's always been you.
you make me feel more like myself
than I ever thought my self could be.
and I don't know what to do with someone
like that,
other than spend the rest of my life with them.
you are why it will never work with anyone else
and why I would never want it to."

*(sometimes what you want is exactly what
you need)*

when he kissed her
he smoothed the edges of the broken pieces
and slowly started putting them back together
where they didn't quite fit or a part was missing
he gave her what she needed to be whole again.
he didn't rip off pieces of himself to stuff into
the cracks
he wrapped his arms around her and reassured
her
made her laugh and held her hand
told her what she did to him and how he felt
about her
treated her like she was both strong and fragile
he loved her as she healed
and she was better than she'd ever been before.

(is this what a healthy relationship is like?)

I'd hate you
but that would require more energy
than I'm willing to expend.

*(even though he's gone, he still shows up in my
words)*

they say that time stops when you kiss
the person you're meant to be kissing
your last first kiss
but when something stops, there's a
sense of an ending
of a finite distinction between all of the
things around you
the sense that whatever comes next will be
separate and unrelated.
when you kissed me,
everything ran together
like the most beautiful blurs of color
grey concrete buildings, yellow cabs, the pink
and purple of the setting sky
when you kissed me, time was suspended
as if everything held its breath
while we somehow stepped outside the
natural laws
and for just a moment
made our very own reality, where anything
was possible
when we went our separate ways, time exhaled
the world around us let out the breath it had
been holding
everything continued on
changed forever by our moment in time
so that nothing would be the same again

Drowned Relief

and it's freezing and it's pretty
this blackness that surrounds me,
pouring down my throat
before it overwhelms my lungs —

I can't breathe but it's familiar
this choking, cloying feeling,
swelling up against me
sweeping numbness dulls my pain —

I don't want it but I need it
a peaceful shadowed drowning,
held inside those arms
engulfed in silent, cruel relief

*(depression. apathy. numbness. I just want
someone to hold me)*

I have the unsettling urge
to go board a plane
and escape everything
I thought I wanted
and am mostly glad I have

*(I have no idea how to
handle life when it's going well)*

Dear Diary,

When someone tells you to keep sending them date ideas because they want to take you to everything you love, you just sit there for a minute, trying to absorb it, even as the words feel like water, sliding off your skin when you climb out of the pool. You replay the words over and over, hearing them in his voice...and question if anyone really, truly, ever loved you before this. You feel the ice thawing in some deep corner of your heart, and something starts to shift...and it's scary, but you're also okay with it. The sexiest, sweetest, most unsettling words I've ever read... "I want to take you to everything you love."

Burned Dissolution

hold me
your fire
consume me
to ashes
burn me and take me for all that I am

hold me
my body
erode me
bones scalding
catch me and make me a part of your light

hold me
I'm melting
devour me
your flames
grab me and strip me of all that's not you

hold me
my essence
remake me
blaze scorching
ignite me, inferno, dissolve me to you

Thanksgiving Poem

when you feel smothered
even though everyone is giving you the space
you never asked for
but probably needed
and you're certain they resent giving it to you
even though they never said as much

when you struggle with questions you want
to ask
because they'll result in answers you don't want
to hear
when you feel alone in the midst of the people
you love
and just can't make sense of everything
even though everything is the best it's been in
so very long

when you don't want to think or feel
you just want to lose yourself in something else,
anything
just so you don't have to try and make sense
of things
that very well may not make sense

(why couldn't I have met you sooner?)

forever started
without warning
so I shouldn't
have been surprised
when it ended
all at once

*(with a police officer standing in my living room,
saying, "we found his body." after a week in the
inpatient psych unit for a suicide attempt.
after another week of being gone without
responding to a single text or call.)*

"just be yourself"
he tells me
then he's shocked
when I breathe fire

what did he expect from a dragon?
and why did I drown my flames?

(don't let anyone drown your flames)

your lies are the only thing
holding my breaking heart together

now I need them
like I once needed you

*(when he promises you that you're the only woman
for him...other than that nasty porn habit)*

why is there something in my head
that refuses to press the "record" button
when you say nice things to me?
it's like when I play back the tracks
there are long pauses of silence
and even though I tell myself
that those are times you're saying things I've
always wanted to hear
I can't make myself hear the words
like I purposefully cut them out or didn't
capture them
to drive home the point I expect to have made
eventually
that the things you tell me are lies
and I'm better off knowing how this is going
to end

(I'm so messed up)

and then, in that moment
when you can look back on how broken
you were
you also realize how far you've come

and it's a realization that hits you like a gale
force wind
almost knocking you over
with the strength of its intensity

I settled for so much less than I deserved
because
I didn't know any better
I thought my worth was equal to whatever
others set it at
I didn't know that my value was mine to set,
and mine alone

it's so painful seeing where I was
but there's also true happiness in seeing how
far I've come
I'll never go back

(never)

healing is so heavy
getting better, recovering
weighs a ton

fuck

ignorance is weightlessness
light and free and soaring above it all
never mind that the only reason you don't
notice the chains that bind you
is because they're featherlight and extend to
unimaginable lengths

so, what will it be —
light enough to fly in prison,
or heavy enough to sit on the ground in
freedom?

you wouldn't think it'd be such a hard choice

*(I ultimately chose freedom. it just took me
10 years)*

I hate the holidays
even though some stubborn part of me refuses
to get in on the act
calling up images of happy holidays
making paper ribbon chains
moving the toy bear on the cloth countdown
calendar
and adding pieces to that lovely hand-carved
manger
but for every happy memory
two or three not-so-happy thoughts arise
not bursting forth like a rocket
but unfurling with languid purpose
like a flower opening its petals
and then I remember why I hate the holidays

(family. more to come on that)

the loneliness surprises me
I've never felt more alone
than driving through town
at night
past all the large houses
with their Christmas lights shining
even though I know most families in those houses
are just as messed up as mine —
still —
it's one thing to be emotionally lonely
it's quite another to be physically alone

you awoke in me
things I didn't even know
were sleeping

*(for the first time in my life,
I find myself liking surprises)*

and once upon a time
the woman with scars
was a girl
whose soul hadn't bled

(still can't shake the cutting)

when it's all said and done
it'll be us
still standing
hand in hand
amidst the rubble of a world
that burned as it refused to believe
our love burned hotter than fire

scooping up the fallen pieces of my
shattered soul
my arms aren't large enough to hold all the
clinking shards
I pick up one and another falls
I rush to grab it, slicing my finger tips to
red-tinted ribbons
"I forget how fragile you are"
he says softly, bewildered at how I fight
to keep myself together
using only my will, I lift my head
and drag my gaze to meet his —
tears stream from my eyes
as blood drips from my hands —
this is what I am now.
I don't even care about being whole
I'm just a body trying to contain
quick-silver slivers of a broken soul
I will never be who I once was
but maybe
with time
and him
I can be better

(not being judged is so incredibly healing)

"sometimes you run
just to see if I'll chase you
and I always will."
I smile and press my face against his neck
so he can't see the disbelief
spreading through my eyes
I have no doubt he means what he says
I only doubt how long
"always" means to him

I wish I'd never learned how to run

(this will continue to be a problem)

My Moment

every now and then
there comes a moment
that you know is different

a miniature fault line
that cracks the span of time
and carves a canyon
across the flat surface
of the clock face

that's what you gave me —
a moment of my very own

(Christmas, 2017)

scars not only alter your skin –
they reshape your soul, as well

*(first-hand knowledge from a
mostly former cutter)*

he held my heart
and raised it to the light

I winced, seeing only
every pulsing, jagged crack

he smiled, seeing only
the light reflecting outwards
shimmering as it kissed
my shattered insides

*(it's all a matter of perspective. find someone
who sees you as the beautiful, precious creature
you are)*

you are
more
than I ever thought
I'd have

summoned into solidity
a jarring strum
across the strings of my being
conjured by the force of your call
awakened
dragged into a new form
by the sheer will of a shared soul
we will always come back together
we are bound
in this occasionally
interrupted
eternity

*(I never believed in soulmates before, although
I secretly always wanted to)*

anyone can love the light
so eager to be seen, to share
few have time for that which conceals
offering nothing except its existence
perhaps real love is embracing the darkness

(I have a lot of darkness)

as tears streamed down my face
I made a noise that might have
been the sound of my heart
breaking

*(when I realized that the pain of staying was
worse than the fear of leaving and that this
would require action on my part)*

I catch a glimpse of her sometimes
from the corner of my eye
the girl I used to be
the girl I want to be again

*(we're finally back on speaking terms. sometimes
she even comes out and stays for a while)*

he looked at me
like I was made of
magic
and
starlight
and fairy dust.
in his eyes, I was

(once you've had someone look at you like this,
you'll never settle for anything less)

I will love you
until the last star
falls from the heavens
and dies in a violent burst
of beautiful flame

and then
I will love you
as we sit in the darkness
and wait
for new worlds to emerge

moonlight covers my skin
and stirs the fallen galaxies
that lie waiting
pulsing
in my veins

(moon. stars. night. home)

your eyes burn away
my insecurities
is it too much to ask
that you gaze at me
until all my fears are ash?

*(I wish I could do this on
my own, but I need help)*

I wanted to be
someone's
first priority
so I became one —

mine.

(better late than never)

the words I've said a thousand times
fail
at describing feelings
I've never felt before

before you

words help me
hold on to things
that are otherwise
too delicate
for my grasp

I am fire
you are happy when I wreak
havoc on some things
yet you rage when I destroy others
I do not discriminate
my nature is to consume, not question
you do not ask why water drowns
so neither ask why I burn

*(don't let anyone try to change your true nature.
it won't work, and it won't be a pleasant   .
experience)*

65

Solid Expression

I've always been looking for ways to express
myself
poetry was the language I could speak without
voice
pouring my soul onto paper
watching it come to life
no longer so ephemeral, but permanent and
seen.

maybe I just wanted proof that I existed
that something was real.
so much around me growing up wasn't
but the words I wrote
the parts of me I cut away and refashioned with
pencil and paper
those let me know that there was a solidity to
life
even if I had to create it myself.

*(family again. everyone did the best they could.
there was love. but it wasn't enough)*

Childhood (?)

the canopy over the bed
       comes down

the Barbie dolls
       are stored in bins under the bed

My Little Ponies
       locked in plastic stalls

while He-Man and She-Ra
       collect dust in the attic

did I purposefully put away my childhood
       or was it taken from me?

did I ever really have it to begin with?
       or were those toys my attempt to be
       the child
       I never felt I was?

*(I have always felt so much older than my actual,
chronological age)*

I filled my ears with the sounds of applause
when I just wanted to hear you say my name
I focused my eyes on papers and letters
when I wanted to be gazing, unblinking, at you
I buried my heart under the weight of
achievements
when I dreamed each night of placing it gently
in your hands

*(don't accept poor substitutions for what you
really want)*

all she wanted
was to be
wanted
accepted
included
for someone to think of her
before she had to remind them
of her existence

(why is this so hard? I don't feel like it should be)

when I met you:
"What luck!" said Chance.
"At last," said Fate.

(co-conspirators in guiding my life)

I throw myself against the bars
of this self-imposed prison
who am I protecting?
and what will it take for me
to finally
let myself out?

(I am my own worst enemy)

the fairytale was a nightmare
you shattered my illusions
then came for the rest of me
leaving me for dead
amidst the what-ifs and whys
and the how-can-this-be-happenings?
but I was stronger than we both thought
I survived
and this time I'm not the damsel
I'm the dragon
and my flames are coming
for every lie you ever told me

*(it's taking a while to burn up what you left in
my mind, but I'm nothing if not persistent)*

some days I'd honestly rather live
secure
in a hell I conjured

than wait for my worst fears to
come true
in a heaven I can't control

*(for a person with major trust issues, nothing
is more important than security. I tend to go
after it any way I can. this is also going to be a
problem)*

charged glimmers
flashes of recognition
inexplicable, magnetic
pulling us toward
what we agreed on
when the stars were
just learning to shine

Oasis of Words

pour words of life
into my parched desert soul
and eventually the sand
will give way to grass
eventually I will be quenched

and some day
long past eventually
I will not only crave such words
from you
I will learn how to say them
to myself

(worth practicing)

there are some criticisms that stay with you
forever
they take away parts of you
you didn't even know you had
enough of these in childhood and
eventually all that's left
is a quiet, somber girl
with eyes that drink in everything
my mind couldn't process the inconsistencies
and the burden was too heavy for my
shoulders.

remember
the bird has to
succumb to the flames
before the Phoenix
can rise
from the ashes

*(I've always been simultaneously
fascinated by/fearful of fire)*

sometimes one touch is all we need
to remind us
that we aren't alone
other times
one touch is all it takes
to remind us
just how alone we've been
how alone we are

*(I do very well in a crisis. it's afterward that I
fall apart, when I look back on what I actually
went through)*

and that's where he was wrong.
because I knew exactly how much I was worth.
I could even reduce it to a handful of
numbers —
the number of tears I had cried.
the number of nights I had lain there, unable
to sleep,
blaming myself.
the number of lies he'd told,
and the number of promises he'd broken.
the number of times I had begged and
screamed and pleaded
with him
to just tell me why.

yes, I knew exactly how much I was worth.
and that's why it was time to leave.

*(however you arrive at the information, knowing
your own worth is priceless)*

Forward Future Walk

it's fine.
it all worked out.
everything ended up being okay.
in fact, things are better than I
ever could have imagined.
I know that now.
but I didn't know it back then.
And that's why I'm crying —
for the girl who couldn't predict
the future,
but kept walking toward it
anyway.

(how on earth did I do everything I did?)

as a child
I wish I'd known
that I was enough
in any given moment
and that my job in growing up
was learning to accept myself
rather than learning
how to change myself
to make everyone around me
happy

(deep down, I'm still conditioned to be
a people pleaser)

hold me so tight
that
not a single fear
can
slip between us

(because I promise you, they're going to try)

once upon a time
I handed around my heart
with abandon
thinking it was something to be shared
rather than
guarded
it's now quite well-protected
but I paid dearly —
security cost me innocence

(I regret so many of the things I traded)

what is it about
the combination
of moonlight and your arms
that calls forth my secrets?
they rise to my eyes
and rest on my lips
waiting to be freed
to be shared
and believed

as a child
I was certain
that the words I wrote
created worlds

no one told me otherwise

(at least not until later)

(I lived in the stories I wrote)

if anyone had told me
what I'd have to go through
to be with you
I'm not sure I would have been
brave enough to face it
but now that I'm with you
and I've seen how brave I can be
I've changed my view of myself
and I will never be without you again

*(we get through things because we have to. it's not
always worth it in the end. but this time, it was)*

my eyes never learned to lie
with quite the same skill
as my mouth
I think people would have seen
the truth in my gaze
if they'd only bothered to
look at me

(but why would they, unless they were clapping
for my latest academic achievement or
complimenting how well-behaved I was?)

she was too scared to take up space
taking up space meant being noticed
and being noticed meant being disapproved of
in every way that mattered
to her fragile child's heart
so she learned to exist between spaces
thinner than a shadow
less noticeable than clear glass
she learned to live while holding her breath
and only let it out sometimes
those times when she was
alone

*(nothing makes you physically disappear like
bulimia and low self-esteem)*

be very careful
lighting the candle
of my broken heart
once I start to burn
we may both
go up in flames

(I don't mean to sound
threatening. please, don't leave)

it was only as
I watched myself
slip away
that I realized
I was worth saving

*(please find ways to let people, especially children,
know how valuable they are. may they never find
themselves slipping away in the first place,
in need of being saved)*

Reignited

for so long
my eyes held nothing but ashes
chalky remnants
of pain and regret
but now
a fire is burning
and the flames are spreading
drying the tears
and clearing out debris
allowing me to finally
see clearly again

*(and I see that there is still
so much good in the world)*

sometimes my tears
form the words
my lips can't

I will love you for as long as I'm able to say
the words…
as long as I'm able to kiss your lips…
as long as I'm able to stroke your face
and run my fingers through your hair.
and if I get to where I can't do those things,
I'll love you in quietness and stillness,
letting my soul nestle against yours.

(I'm ready for a love without end)

we wake from the nightmare
only to carry the memories of
what we saw
with us
my brain is never better at
remembering
than when it comes to the things
I most want to forget

*(me replaying traumas in my dreams is going
to be a common theme that doesn't end on the last
page of this book)*

no matter how often life tells me otherwise
my heart still finds reasons to hope
(check back later to see
how that works out for me)

*(I am cynical and suspicious and jaded, but even
so, some small part of me is still an irrepressible
optimist. I'm mostly glad)*

sometimes at night
I walk out and look up
at the stars
it's nice to feel seen
when you're lonely

(do the stars feel lonely? do they come out to watch
us? things I wondered as a child)

in the stillness
the outside world is out of focus
and the only thing I'm aware of
is the rise and fall of our shared breathing
creating a space where we meet
merging
no distinction between where you end
and I begin
and I might be scared of losing myself
if it didn't feel so familiar
if I couldn't trace the lines of your soul
from memories
I have no memory of making

in the forest of my childhood
I was terrified of meeting a creature
from my nightmares
thankfully, I never did
but
in the forest of my grown-up mind
the monsters wait for me
always there
I know each one by name

*(it's hard to truly hate the things that are
always so excited to see me)*

do this
not that
go here
not there
a little more
not so much
hurry up
not so fast

(a summary of growing up)

when I say "I miss you"
I'm not just talking about how I feel
since the last time I saw you
I'm talking about how I felt
all those years I wasn't with you
and should have been

*(the part of me that got along without you for so
long still can't believe we're really together)*

take my hand
those places that you never
thought you'd go
we'll visit together
uncomfortable
uncertain
uncharted
to be sure
I don't know what to expect
but I promise
to never let go of your hand

(we can get through anything together)

your arms are around me
but I'm huddled in a corner
head down, knees to my chest
I can't stop the tears but I can silence the sobs
neither your words nor your touch
can calm my fears
for being so close we're so far apart
with an impenetrable barrier between us
an unscalable wall constructed from
my past experiences
each brick held together by the invisible mortar
of my inability to trust
and even though I know it's not true
everything in me tells me I'm alone
that I should run, hide, protect myself
and although some part of me wants to stay
I'm already leaving, retreating,
finding refuge in the furthest corner of
my mind

(and there I go, running again)

once upon a time there lived a girl with soft brown eyes and an even softer heart. she didn't choose to be this way. she just was.

she didn't fit into the world in which she found herself. when she was warm, it was cold. when she was kind, it was cruel.

and she found herself hurt again and again and again.

she tried to harden her heart, but she couldn't. so, she locked it away for safe keeping.

she learned to blend in to the cruelness around her. and those soft brown eyes became hard as flint, keeping the world at a distance and protecting her scared, lonely self.

(I wish I could go back in time, hug my younger self, and tell her that someday she'll learn it's possible to be both strong and vulnerable. someday she'll learn that there are people worthy of her trust)

my dear, you have no idea
how fast I can retreat
into my mind
one look, one word, one laugh
and I'm gone
running deeper into the familiar
chaotic darkness
I say I want to be free of

*(knowing I can't run away from my issues has
never kept me from trying)*

I shrugged my cape-covered shoulders and held the wolf's unblinking gaze.

"it's just that you're not the most terrifying creature I've ever come across," I said.

he squinted his yellow eyes, clearly taken aback.

"you're still quite frightening," I added, wanting to reassure him. "It's just that, here, in this part of the forest, I expect to meet things that scare me. the worst monsters are the ones you never suspect…the ones who take advantage of the fact that you depend on them."

I swallowed hard and whispered, "the real monsters aren't the ones I can run away from… they're the ones I go home to."

(I still find this brutally uncomfortable to share, but I feel like that's exactly why I need to…for other people who don't find safety, whatever that looks like, at home)

the lure of the moon is too great
and so, I walk on
desperate to be near something
that gazes at me
with such undivided attention

(for all I write about needing attention,
I can't ever imagine actually saying those words
to someone. I guess I just hope they'll notice?)

why is it here
at the edges of my mind
that I feel calm?
the madness lies waiting
I appreciate its patience
I suppose I've proven
that I'll always come back

*(there is so much comfort to be drawn from
the familiar)*

only with you
do I feel safe enough
to be me

(and I like who I am when I'm with you)

Hotel Room

and she takes another step
closes the door softly behind her
faded carpet, scratchy sheets,
a tv, and two locks to hide she's here
the tears will start again
but right now it's only anger
and relief at getting away
and pretending that she won't answer
when he calls to know where she is
another sleepless night
paying for a few hours to herself
a chance to imagine she's free
here she can pretend she's safe
that she won't be thinking tomorrow
of lies to explain his behavior
she wishes someone knew
that a knock on the door would save her
but that would be the only thing
worse than going back
driving the empty, well-worn road
leading home to her broken life.

(parts of my marriage I never told anyone about)

Repeated Drownings

I have drowned so many times:
in the silence between us
in the loneliness of avoiding shared spaces
in the emptiness of sleeping alone
in the lies I eventually stopped unraveling
in the tears I refused to cry
in the words I couldn't speak
in the fear that panted against my neck for
months
in the gulf between who I was and who I
wanted to be
and most recently, in his eyes.

Soul Recognition

I've traveled galaxies to find you
cut through currents of light-years to reach you
circled the darkness of obsidian holes
for the chance to be back in your arms
how many times have we done it
traded our pasts in exchange for a present?
going through life asleep, in a fog,
searching for what we can't even name

until

the time of awakening arrives
our attention becomes wholly arrested
that instant, breath-stopping recognition
when the half of my soul
housed in your body
calls out to me in welcome

(persistence, rewarded)

The Fate of Soulmates

how long have we done this?
the forced spaces we tolerate
when we aren't together
the cosmic payment for
the indescribable joy
we drown in
when we're finally
reunited
it's impossible, transcending these
boundaried limitations
yet we do it, and we always will
overcoming, overturning
bending all else around us
guided by our own gravitational pull

(impossible doesn't apply to us)

Lost & Put Back Together

I lost myself
somewhere between
willful ignorance
youthful optimism
and practiced lies
I eventually escaped
unlocking my restraints
with the keys I'd hidden in my pocket
I traveled back along the path of loss
collecting the cast-off pieces of my soul
until, back at the very beginning,
I had collected all of myself.

It was time to put me together again.

(it's an ongoing process, but I can see progress)

Interludes

interludes
those moments between anxiety
when you forget how worried you are
and feel as if you're finally moving
at the same pace
as the rest of the world
and then just as you're appreciating the break
you're thrown back into your normal state
where the only thing racing faster than your
heart
is your mind
and you are painfully aware
of just how messed up you are

*(sometimes I think my life is just one long
experience of feeling so different from other
people)*

there was no glass slipper
no knight in shining armor
no fairy godmother, no magic spell
there was no rescue
there was only a girl
and the decisions she made
she stopped eating poison apples
and wore gloves when she used the spinning
wheel
with the help of a dragon
she set the castle on fire
and left the enchanted forest
without a single backward glance

she also lived happily ever after

(and wrote her own ending)

someday
someone won't think you're
too much of something –
too complicated
too difficult
too hard to handle
or too exhausting

someday
someone will see that you're exactly right
just the way you are
and someone will love you and accept you
without conditions or hesitations

make sure that someone
is you

when the past overwhelms me
and I am bent, broken
my eyes cast down
sit with me in the darkness
and tell me about the stars
until we are both able to see them

(the best way to help me)

once upon a time
in a faraway land
there lived a little girl

who wanted something so precious
it was only rarely given out
by the people around her

this treasure she so desperately wanted —

time

(spend your time, not your money,
on the people you care about)

once smooth wings
now disfigured by scars
gossamer webbing dulled,
worn thin,
torn from careless handling

such beautiful adornments
accustomed to soaring

they were never meant
to be battle armor

(the transformation of Dark Fairy)

the soft hands of my nightmare
slip gently around my wrists
pulling me slowly downward
into horrors
remembered and imagined
the things I can most depend on
are the things I want to avoid
waiting for me
night after night
as soon as I close my eyes

(I hate to sleep alone)

on this day
all those years ago
I didn't know it
but I was waiting for you

(the timing was finally right)

Living on Eggshells

come, sit with me in the hayloft
with my mud-spattered Keds
and faded red jeans
long straight hair frames cautious brown eyes
that are much too old for my face
let me show you the story I'm writing
where the ending will always be happy
here, we're forgotten
hidden away
safe from the madness without

now, I'll sit with you under the stairs
in a fort made of pillows
with a plaid blanket roof
the glow from the flashlight shows guarded
blue eyes
that are much too old for your face
show me the comic you're reading
where good always wins in the end
here, we're invisible
hidden away
safe from the madness without

*(a basic, foundational reason we understand
one another)*

I gave away so much
that I didn't even realize had been mine
it wasn't until I started taking things back
that I realized what had once
been in my possession
precious things
and I had lost them
given them away
let them be taken from me
traded them for promises that never became
more than painful regrets

never again.

*(lesson learned. I wish I could protect other girls
from going through anything similar)*

I quit.
I quit trying to pretend I'm not sensitive
I quit staying quiet when people said things
that made me uncomfortable
I quit hiding the parts of myself I worried
others wouldn't like
I quit pasting a smile on my face
when I didn't feel happy
and I quit believing I was automatically
to blame if something went wrong
once I quit doing these things
then
I was finally able to start living

*(some days I'm more successful at quitting than
others, but this is always the goal)*

even after all this time
I still find myself wanting to tell you things
big, important, life-changing events
and small, inconsequential,
everyday happenings
it would almost be easier if you weren't here
if there were a better reason I don't tell you
things
than simply the pitiful quality of our
relationship
I don't really know how we devolved to this
and even though I have to live with it
I don't know that I'll ever stop wishing it was
different
that we were different

*(mother/daughter relationships are complicated
in my family)*

do you not realize by now
that I hang on every word you say
that it sticks in my mind
carves itself into my neurons
to be replayed over and over and
over again?
I wish you could understand
the power your words have
maybe then
you wouldn't throw them around
like confetti
making messes
I'll never fully clean up

*(it would be so much easier if things didn't
affect me so deeply)*

when I close my eyes
I'm finally able to see
the secrets I want to hide from the sunlight
the hopes that get overwhelmed by the
demands
the fears I don't want to face during the day
and the pain that's forced to wait in the
darkness
only when I'm blind to everything
around me
do I truly begin to see

how do we emerge
victorious
from the still-smoking ashes
of our charred pasts?
how do series of events
conspire together to make us
into the people we are now?
we are the sum of our experiences
but also so much more

*(people amaze me every day at
what they're able to overcome)*

I can't decide what hurts worse
losing the parts of me
you take with you when you go
or keeping the parts of me
that are forced to stay behind
every time you leave
I'm never fully here
but I'm never fully gone
there's no equilibrium to be found
and my constant attempts at balance
are maddening

(long-distance is not sustainable)

why can't I be like everyone else?
why can't I just fit in?
I didn't ask to be different
people say "special" or "unique"
like those are good things
but they're not
I don't want to be the center of attention
or the reason people stop talking
when I walk in the room
why do I feel like a problem that can't
be solved
or like the last living member
of an otherwise extinct species
why am I cursed with these wings
when I'm terrified of heights
and have no desire to fly?

(my life for as long as I can remember)

sunshine laughter laced with worry
cotton candy facts spun into truth
skipping didn't suit me but dragging my feet
meant scuffing my new shoes
I pulled my friends from books
and hoped being me was only an act
when I couldn't ask questions
smiles kept the words
locked behind closed teeth
and little by little
or sometimes all at once
being perceptive stole my innocence
and cost me a carefree childhood

*(why couldn't I have been oblivious and happy,
rather than seeing that things weren't right but
not being able to talk about them?)*

I want your yesterdays
your somedays
your tomorrows
and your now

(my nature is all-consuming)

and ultimately at the end of the day
it's me
I'm the one I have to depend on
maybe it's just perpetually bad timing
but when crises come
I'm always alone
so I do what I always do
I get through them
alone.

perhaps I am cursed
to navigate trials on my own
but blessed
with the strength to do so.

*(while this is true, it's not the whole truth.
not anymore)*

everyone else is gone
it's quiet
too quiet
but thankfully I'm not alone for long
slowly my demons emerge from the shadows
one of them hugs me
another wipes away my tears
"We can make you feel better," they whisper
they're not wrong
they will, even if part of me will regret it
but right now, I'll choose regret over loneliness

*(it's hard to hate the things that have been with
me through thick and thin, even if their advice
means new scars, visible or invisible, on some part
of me)*

falling through the sky
from my white-knuckled perch on cloud nine
it was a slow sort of crash
and I watched the ground rise up to meet me
ready to shatter the illusions
I insisted on maintaining
it wasn't until I pushed myself up
and surveyed the mess around me
that I realized I didn't want
to put the pieces back together
so I dragged my broken, bruised, cut-up self
away
a mess
but one who was free to walk and run
no more sitting still, holding my breath,
afraid to move
watching life happen below me

*(choose freedom. choose yourself. make your life
your own)*

in my lowest times
I gave control of myself over to my demons
and they protected me
now that times are good
they don't understand why I need them
to go away
what once kept me safe
is now wreaking havoc

(I'm having to learn new coping skills)

Silent Speech

some days even the best words will never
be enough
there will be times when nothing you say
will reassure me or convince me
that everything's going to be fine
when I can't hear you, just sit with me in
the silence
and put your hand on mine
speak with your touch
so that my heart may listen
to everything my ears ignore

Song of Renewal

come ancient healer
sing over this parched pile of bones
this bleached heap of broken promises
lying forgotten, waiting for renewal
let your words of life fall soft on the
carcass of the creature I once was
awakening
assuring
and assembling
making soul solid
as I linger, longing,
waiting for transformation
hoping I am meant to live

(and I will. in a life of my own making)

it gets discouraging some days
looking at how far I have to go
to become the person I want to be

but then I look back on how far I've come
how different I am
from the person I used to be

and I remember that I can do this
because I'm already doing it
change is a process
not just a clearly defined event

(I wish this wasn't so hard for me to remember)

he forgot about me
when we lived in the same house
why should I think you'll remember me
when I'm not around?

(it's a fair question)

you are the sun
and I am in desperate need of your light
without it I'm alone
unable to keep from slipping into madness
lost in the dark
shine on me
warm me through to my cooled, dormant cells
seep into my bones and flood my soul
bring me back to life

(I need you. more than I care to admit)

fear drives out
every other thought in my head
it drowns my hopes
my best intentions
and skews everything so that
I don't know what's real and
what's not anymore

*(this is a terrifying way to live.
I hope it gets better.)*

one of the most important decisions
you'll ever make
is whether or not to accept yourself

*(how you feel about yourself is something no one
can ever take away from you. there is so much
power in that)*

alone in my room
my refuge
my sanctuary
the walls don't confine me
they embrace me
here I explore
here I understand
here I can extend the wings
that no one knows I have
here I am me without judgment

(childhood origins of Dark Fairy)

there are things inside of me
I've pushed down and ignored
because I wasn't sure I could handle them
they scared me because they were different
but now little by little
they're coming out
and I'm learning to draw my power from
things
I would have previously denied possessing

(this is a very good change of events)

as your fingertips brushed my face
they gently soothed my unquiet soul

*(the power of touch to heal wounds that can't
be seen)*

why?
why should I be quiet?
why do I have to be the one who calms down?
what is it about me that means I have to listen?
to be reasonable?
because that makes it easier for you to
categorize me?
control me?
to put me in a place that leaves you feeling
secure in your false superiority?
I'm not here to make things easier for you
and I'm done pretending otherwise

*(when a woman decides she's done letting men
run her life)*

I wish I could borrow your eyes
even for just a few minutes
I'd look at myself in the mirror
and try to see the person you tell me I am

(someday I'll believe the words you tell me)

it's easy to be in awe of fire
it's a powerful force
causing strong metals to weaken
when subjected to its flames
it fills the darkest sky
brighter than the glow of distant galaxies
flames dance with heated abandon
indiscriminate in consumption
hypnotic in burning beauty
yet for all this
there is one thing fire can never do
and that is be held
I wonder if it ever gets lonely
admired, but always kept at arm's length?

*(in case it's not obvious, fire is a metaphor for me.
sometimes I feel incapable of being held. of being
happy. of being in a relationship)*

when going places has a magic all of its own
and you count down the days leading up to
something important
when the smallest things are discussed in the
greatest detail
because everything that happens has
lasting significance

(the threshold of adolescence)

by the time I reach the end of this tale
written every day with the ink of experience
I will have played every role in the story

(hero. villain. savior. destroyer. and everything
in between)

the house feels as empty as my heart
I'm lost
listening for sounds I'll never hear again
surrounded by reminders I'm sure will one day
make me smile
sadness has taken your place as my constant
companion
as I move through this foreign world
of learning to live without you

*(first day of life without my dog, Dante, who was
my life for almost 11 years)*

hold me close
let your hands reassure me
in ways that words never will
kiss away my fears
and remind me why needing someone
isn't such a bad thing

(I'm sorry that I need so much reminding)

when a heart breaks
it never gets put back together
quite the same way it was before
pieces are missing
edges don't line up
these painful reconfigurations
are the shape of loss
but they are also
the shape of love
we are changed by the things we care about

*(in being changed by the things we love,
they never truly leave us)*

there is a place we go
that we can only find when
we suspend disbelief
when thinking is replaced by feeling
and we let ourselves fall into the between
where we meet
together
an eternity removed from everything else
where we are all that's in focus
and we live lifetimes in our shared created space

sometimes there are no words
and pain isn't expressed
it is merely endured

*(knowing we will get through something doesn't
make it any easier)*

some dreams are so fragile
some hopes so small
that we're scared to even think about them
afraid that too much attention will make
them disappear
leaving us worse off than if we'd never dared
to think such thoughts in the first place

*(fear doesn't have to stop you. another lesson I
wish I would have learned sooner)*

I've worn this armor for so long
that I don't even know
when I first put it on
but then you touched me
and I remembered —

my skin wasn't always made of metal

(surprising realization)

I was forged in star fire
and cooled in the winds of a hurricane
I have been battered and beaten and pummeled
shaped by the forces around me
yet still, I stand
somewhere within me I feed on
chaos and destruction
you, therefore, underestimate
what it will take to break me

(I underestimated me, too, but never again)

I tuck the night around me
like a blanket
and spread a mask of stars
over my eyes
here in this infinite space
we meet
here in this backlit darkness
we remember
here
we will always be together

just because she isn't broken
doesn't mean she isn't fragile

*(the danger of being strong is that people
sometimes forget you're also damaged. the two
aren't mutually exclusive)*

I fought to be the person I am today
come, walk a mile in my memories
before you tell me how I ought to be

(enough said)

life has a way of shaking the towers
you thought were secure
until they lie in pieces
broken stones scattered in piles
and you're left unprotected
surrounded by chaos with nothing you
can depend on
except yourself
and that's when you gather the pieces
of the life you lost
and use them to build the life you want

*(build the life you want because no one else is
going to do it for you)*

sometimes I wonder what my soul must
look like
after all I've been through
I imagine it started off
neat and slick and smooth
flat
without a single scratch or bump
and then over time
on the other side of experience
it changed
and now I imagine it looks like land
devastated by an earthquake
as seen from the sky above
marked by cracks and craters and spots where
you can tell it was healing
before another tectonic shift
ripped it apart again

(also known as 'life')

moonlight softens the edges
of even the sharpest pain
perhaps that is why I come alive at night
lured from my dormant state
I can tolerate otherwise unimaginable hurts
then, I can even stand the ache of being myself

*(it still hurts to read this, but the passage of time
doesn't change the truth of what I felt at that
moment)*

we may not get to choose the beginning,
since all stories start out the same:

"Once upon a time, there lived…"

so it's up to each of us to write our own ending
to make it different
unique
our own

*(such responsibility can be daunting. creating is
not always easy, even if it's rewarding)*

we watch the world with smoke-filled eyes
but every now and then
a breeze comes along
in the form of unexpected kindness
and clears our clouded view

(I'm queen of the clouded view. in spite of,
or perhaps because of, this, I'm always deeply
appreciative of genuine kindness)

wrap your arms around my broken spirit
hold the shards of my shattered dreams in
your hands
polish every fractured piece of me until I shine
until I no longer fear being damaged beyond
all repair

*(I feel like I never know the right amount to
expect. I either expect too much or too little, and
neither one is fair to you)*

and in the end
does it matter how we got here?
that it was unconventional and unexpected and
something we could never explain?
no
the most important part is that we're together
finally and forever

*(some parts of our history will always be
inexplicable, and I'm fine with that)*

I just want to be enough for someone
for you
but also for myself

*(this is a constant theme in my life, so I'm not
surprised that it keeps showing up on these pages)*

I will never be tame
domesticated
with no desire to revel in my
otherworldly power
I can, however, be persuaded
that your arms are worth forgoing
the safety of my isolation
and I think that choosing to stay because
you give me a reason
is better than having no desire to leave
in the first place

(in theory, domesticity and wildness can coexist.
in practice, this will be a struggle with each
side fighting for dominance)

experience has taught me that
"I love you"
is just a nicer way of saying
"I'll eventually leave you"
yet there is still some part of me
that continues to hope
maybe this time
with you
it might mean something different

(the part of me that's an eternal optimist
rears her head again)

as our eyes met
everything that had once kept us apart
was no more
each step forward took me further from
my past
and closer to exactly what I'd wanted for
so long
the years slipped behind me
burning to ash in the electricity
humming ever louder between us
and as I finally felt your lips against mine
it was almost as if we'd never been apart

*(what's meant to be will find a way. I didn't
really believe this until I started experiencing it)*

summer nights
in late July
he was the sun
and under
his unwavering warmth
she blossomed

(best summer of my life)

once upon a time
I dreamed of happily ever after
but only when I realized that
I alone am responsible for my own happiness
did I know the ending would turn out happy

(it really is up to you. depending on the day,
this makes me feel either incredibly hopeful
or insanely despondent)

if I had known when I was younger
that I would carry my past with me
forever
always forward into my future
I would have done a great many things
differently

(take that risk. travel more.
care less what others think)

someday you and I will stop apologizing
to each other
for what other people did to us
for who they made us become
for what they turned us into
without us even knowing
someday we'll trust that we are
truly acceptable just as we are
and that we're worthy of being loved
without conditions

(someday...but until then, we'll just keep being
patient with each other)

in the end
I just want someone
who chooses me
every time
over everything else
without hesitation

*(choosing me should never really have to
be a choice)*

and sometimes in the night I meet myself
when I can no longer stay away
drawn forth by the quiet and the darkness
I never know what's going to be revealed
in those moments
but rather than cringing away
I now welcome those encounters
and I'm surprised at how much I like
discovering
parts of myself
that have existed for so long in isolation
it's nice to slowly realize
that all of me belongs

(less self-loathing, more self-love)

there's still time
to become the person
you used to dream
of being

(it's not too late. really.
this one's for you. go for it)

when I look in the mirror
I am both completely the same
and entirely unrecognizable
I'm not who I used to be
I'm finally becoming
who I was meant to be —
I'm finally becoming myself

(own it)

I used to stay awake each night
to wish upon a star
then I met you
now I stay up all night
telling the stars stories of us

as darkness descends
memories rise
floating upwards like air bubbles
seeking the surface of a pond
once they've escaped,
there's no ignoring them or
returning them to the safety of
the confines of my mind
I watch them play out
again and again and again
already knowing the ending
and dreading the journey to get there
sleep is elusive and sadness abundant
in this horror of repetition
I'm trapped in each night

*(yeah, still dealing with those nightmares.
I'd give anything to forget some things)*

I bury myself under so many layers —
layers of clothes
to hide the body I'm insecure about
layers of defenses
to protect my sensitive heart
layers of makeup
to make me look like everyone else
and layers of fake smiles
to hide my fear and doubt

(I just don't want to get hurt. not again)

some days the world is so dark
that you are the only light you'll see
— shine anyway —

(even a small light shines in total darkness)

thank you
for seeing me as I was
while also seeing me
as I could be

*(magical things can happen when someone
sees you exactly as you are and accepts you, with
all your scars and your infinite possibilities)*

there are things I want now
that I never thought I would care about
and there are things that no longer interest me
that I thought I would need forever
time and experience offer new perspectives
if only we are brave enough to open our eyes
and see

*(I'm still working on being brave, but my eyes
are open. and the view is breath-taking.)*

you are not someone to be handled
or tolerated
or put up with until you can learn to be better
you are meant to be cherished
adored
and loved without measure
for exactly who you are
I'm sorry it's taken so many years
for you to learn this
but I'm happy to be the one to show you

(for you, reader. you are enough.
if you take away nothing else from this book,
remember that.)

Afterword

once upon a time there lived a girl
once upon a time her life fell to pieces
once upon a time she built a new life
and she is living happily ever after.

About the Author

Ever since I can remember, I've wanted to be a writer. This is most likely due to the enormous impact books had on me growing up. The stories and poems I read as a child shaped me into the person I am today. They made me feel strong and smart and hopeful. Most of all, they made me feel like I wasn't so alone. That is my goal in sharing my words — to let you know that I've been there (or thereabouts), I see you, and you are not the last surviving member of an otherwise extinct species.

My dream of being a writer was put aside in the name of doing what I thought I "had" to do. Then, in February 2017, my life fell apart, and I had the chance to completely reinvent myself. I decided not to waste any more time going down a career path I didn't truly love, and I decided not to worry about what everyone would say. Having faced my deepest fears and somehow survived, nothing seemed quite as important as being true to myself. So, that's what I'm trying to do.

I'm so grateful you chose to give your attention to this book, and I'd love to hear from you. You can find me on Instagram @darkfairydreams or on Facebook at facebook.com/katiekeridan.

93824192R00111

Made in the USA
San Bernardino, CA
09 November 2018